W9-DHG-659

WHEN A PARENT IS MENTALLY ILL

ALLISON J. ROSS

The Rosen Publishing Group, Inc.
New York

To my family

Published in 2001 by The Rosen Publishing Group, Inc.
29 East 21st Street, New York, NY 10010

First Edition

Cover Photo by Antonio Mari

Library of Congress Cataloging-in-Publication Data

Ross, Allison J., 1974–
Coping when a parent is mentally ill / by Allison J. Ross.—1st ed.
p. cm. — (Coping)
Includes index.
ISBN 0-8239-3359-8
1. Mental illness—Juvenile literature. 2. Mentally ill—Family relationships—Juvenile literature. 3. Children of the mentally ill—Juvenile literature. [1. Mental illness. 2. Parent and child. 3. Family problems.] I. Title. II. Series.
RC460.2 .R67 2001
616.89—dc21

2001000460

Manufactured in the United States of America

Contents

Introduction

We all experience brief periods of confusion, anxiety, or sadness as a normal part of our everyday lives. You may feel anxious when speaking in front of a large group, or you may think that you hear something that no one else heard, or you might feel sad for a few days because your best friend moved away. These are normal, everyday occurrences and normal, everyday emotions.

Mental illness affects the way a person thinks, acts, and feels. With mental illness, the symptoms are intense—so intense that they can interfere with normal functioning. Mental illness can affect sleeping, eating, social relationships, work, and the ability to maintain appropriate behavior. In the United States, one in five people have or will have a mental illness at some point in their lives. About 3 percent, or five million adults, are considered to be suffering from a severe and persistent mental illness. What if one of those five million mentally ill adults is your parent?

Changes in How the Mentally Ill Are Viewed by Society

The medical and popular view of mental illness has changed remarkably over the course of time. In the not-so-distant past, the mentally ill were looked upon and treated as outcasts. They were considered untreatable, and many were locked up in asylums or institutions. Some people believed that those who were mentally ill were possessed by the devil. There was also the belief that the mentally ill were "normal" people with weak morals or eccentricities, and that they chose to "act" mentally ill. In other words, it was thought that a mental illness was something that one could control or choose not to have. Now we know that these beliefs were born out of ignorance, but at the time, there wasn't enough scientific research on the mentally ill to counter these common, but extremely unfair myths.

Beginning in the 1950s, the treatment of the mentally ill underwent a transformation. New drugs (such as chlorpromazine for schizophrenia or imipramine for depression) were found to be of considerable help to sufferers of these illnesses. These drugs were considered to be major breakthroughs—not only did they allow many mentally ill people to find relief and the promise of a more normal life without having to live in institutions, but they also had a positive effect on society's overall understanding of mental illness. Also, research established that biological abnormalities were associated with psychiatric disorders, proving, once and for all, that these illnesses were treatable, and that their sufferers were not possessed by the devil or acting this way on purpose, as was previously thought.

Mental illness is now viewed as a medical affliction instead of being seen as the ultimate taboo illness. With effective treatment, patients can be helped considerably, and many are able to lead productive and comfortable lives.

Mental Illness Knows No Boundaries

Despite the discovery of new treatments, the prevalence of mental illness has not lessened over the years. Mental illnesses continue to affect about 2 percent of all societies, although the figures may vary, depending on how a particular society defines and tolerates mental illness. In other words, some societies are more accepting of those with mental illness, while others have wider definitions of mental illness.

Mental illness knows no boundaries; it does not pick and choose whom it strikes, and it does not seem to prey on any particular age group or racial group. Anyone can suffer from mental illness, and it can strike at any time. Certain illnesses may affect some groups of people more than others, but as a rule, no one is immune from becoming mentally ill.

Wondering Where to Turn

Different people have varying ways of dealing with mental problems. Some, in a misguided effort to medicate themselves or to mask their pain, turn to illegal drugs and/or alcohol. For those living in poverty or for those without health insurance, care is limited. Illiteracy, ignorance, or cultural beliefs about the mind and body may stand in the way of receiving treatment. With awareness, education, and proper treatment, much can be done to alleviate this needless suffering.

You most likely picked up this book because you suspect that a parent (yours or a friend's) is mentally ill. Or perhaps your parent has been diagnosed as having a mental illness, and you wish to learn more about what he or she is going through, and how you can cope with this situation. Whatever the case, you may be experiencing several emotions. Frequently, the offspring of mentally ill parents feel sad, worried, angry, and/or guilty. You will learn that these are all normal emotional responses, and you will discover that you are not alone. There are plenty of available resources—ranging from books to qualified mental health professionals—that can help you through this difficult stage.

The burden of your parent's illness—and yes, it can be a burden—should not fall on you alone. Remember to think about yourself, too. Finding a trusted adult to help you is one of the most important things that you can do. You can also choose to see a therapist and/or attend support group meetings. In the Where to Go for Help section at the back of this book, you will find several listings that will be of use to you in terms of finding a support network or finding a professional who can help you. It is important for you to remember that, as the offspring of a parent who is mentally ill, you need just as much support as your parent does. Seeking help for yourself is not a sign of weakness—it is a sign of strength.

How Can I Tell If My Parent Is Mentally Ill?

As mentioned in the introduction, anyone can be affected by mental illness at any point in time. That said, you may be wondering how you can tell if a parent is suffering from a mental illness—or if he or she is just experiencing a strong and normal reaction to a life crisis. Let's look at the case of Stephanie, who was wondering the exact same thing about a year ago.

Stephanie's Dad: Is He Depressed?

"My father worked as a buyer in a department store. Basically, his job was to choose the items that the store would sell. But after many years of being in business, the company announced that it was losing money, and that it was going to have to make some reductions in staff. None of us thought that my father would lose his job—he had worked there for more than twenty years, and everyone had a lot of respect for him. So when he came home one day and announced that he was laid off, we were all stunned.

"At first, it wasn't that bad. My mother is an elementary school teacher, so we knew that our finances would be okay for awhile. And my dad seemed to be doing pretty well under the circumstances. Right after he was laid off, he would get up early to start job-hunting, and he always helped out around the house. But after a month passed, and then another month, we began to worry about him. He was waking up later and later, and he was always irritable and sad. I was worried that he was depressed, and I wondered if he should get some help."

Three months after losing his job, Stephanie's dad found another one.

"Instantly, his mood changed. He was the same lovable, bright person we were used to. The day he was hired, we all went out for a family dinner to celebrate. My father made a toast, and he apologized for his behavior. 'I know I've been tough to live with over the past couple of months,' he said. 'But losing my job was upsetting. I did not expect it to happen, and it was a job that I really loved. After some time had passed, I began to doubt myself. I even started to wonder if I would ever find another job that I loved as much. But now, I could not be happier, and I could not have done it without the love and support of my family. I want to thank all of you for sticking by me and supporting me—it must have been scary for you.'"

Stephanie looks back on the ordeal with relief that it didn't last too long. "It has been a year since this happened, and during this time, my dad has been the same wonderful person he always was," she says. "I learned that what he was experiencing was not depression at all. He was just sad and upset over the loss of his job, and he felt discouraged over the prospect of finding a new one."

Perhaps your parent is in a similar situation—perhaps you have noticed that your parent's mood or behavior has changed due to a life crisis, physical illness, side effects of medication, or other factors. How do you know if what your parent is suffering from can be classified as a mental illness? The truth is, you don't know. You don't know if the behavior is fleeting, or if it will continue for months or years. And you can't be expected to know, either. If you suspect that your parent might be suffering from a mental illness, you can reach out to an adult you trust. You might also find it helpful to learn more about mental illness and what your parent is going through. Your doctor or another adult can point you in the right direction and guide you to the right resources.

Signs and Symptoms of Mental Illness

As you read this book, you will learn about the different symptoms that are associated with various mental illnesses. Each illness has its own set of signs and symptoms that can serve as hints that an underlying illness may be the cause of certain behavior. Some common warning signs of mental illness include the following:

- A noticeable personality change over time
- Confused thinking
- Strange or grandiose ideas
- Prolonged severe depression, apathy, or extreme highs and lows
- Substance abuse (such as alcohol or illicit drug abuse)
- Withdrawal from society
- Thinking or talking about suicide
- Anger or hostility that is out of proportion to the situation at hand
- Delusions, hallucinations, or hearing voices

Any of these signs can be an indication that your parent is suffering from mental illness. However, it is important that you realize that only a medical professional will be able to tell you for sure.

Depression

We often hear people say that they are depressed. A bad day at work, a rough time with a homework assignment, a fight with a friend—all of these things can lead us to say "I'm depressed." We all tend to feel sad and "down" from time to time—this is a normal reaction to life's upsets and disappointments. But when we use the word depression to describe our bad day at work, we are not referring to a constant, persistent feeling of despondency that has continued for months, and will not go away. You might feel sad for an hour, or a day, or even a week or two—this is normal, and it happens to everyone. Eventually, though, the sad feelings subside, and you are able to return to acting like your usual self.

Clinical Depression—When the Sad Feelings Don't Go Away

In what is known as "clinical" depression, the feelings of sadness and hopelessness do not go away, no matter how hard the depressed person tries to make them disappear, or how much the depressed person wants them to. Instead, the feelings of sadness and despair persist and worsen, ultimately affecting all aspects of that person's life. Some people have described depression as a sort of "black cloud" that hangs over them.

Many people who have not experienced depression are not able to understand it. After all, if a person is sad, why can't he or she just be happy again? Why must depression affect everything he or she does? Why can't he or she control his or her moods like everyone else? Why is it that the depressed person is unable to just "snap out of it"?

Depression is not just a shift in mood or feeling. This illness affects, alters, and disrupts a depressed person's mood, but, as previously mentioned, it also affects many other aspects of life. For example, depression affects one's thoughts, one's body, and one's behavior. The negative feelings persist, and linger, and pervade every movement and action that a depressed person makes. And depression is very common: Approximately 15 million Americans suffer from this illness.

Symptoms of Depression

As previously mentioned, when a person suffers from clinical depression, his or her mood is severely affected. A depressed person feels melancholic and miserable—not some of the time, but most of the time.

Mood

It is difficult for someone who is depressed to feel pleasure about anything, even if it is an activity he or she used to enjoy. It is also difficult for a depressed person to take an active interest in anything, even when it pertains to subjects that the person used to feel passionately about. Consider the case of Janice's mother, who has been suffering from depression for over a year.

Janice's Mother: The Beginning of Depression

"My mother is the manager of a greeting card store," Janice begins. "One of her greatest passions is creating original greeting cards. Over the years, she has made a variety of different cards that include her own drawings, sketches, and poems. A month or two before she started to feel depressed, she enrolled in a watercolor course so that she could take her passion for greeting cards to the next level—eventually selling cards with little watercolors of lighthouses and cottages on them.

"The course was everything my mother had hoped it would be; I had never seen her so happy. She told me that her teacher complimented her on her work and told her that she seemed to have true talent for an activity that many find difficult. She was thrilled. In her spare time—after work and on weekends—my mother would practice what she learned in class. She began designing some cards and was pleased with the results.

"A couple of months into the class, my mom began feeling what she later described as 'blue'—she was just never quite as happy or as enthusiastic as she used to be. My mother began sleeping a lot, and eventually she lost all interest in eating and spending time with her friends. Even her watercolor class—the

class she used to love so much—became a chore. Eventually, she had zero interest in designing her watercolor cards, and she stopped attending class. Not only that, but she said that she couldn't imagine ever wanting to pick up a paintbrush again."

As we can see with Janice's mother, those who are depressed often experience a decrease in energy and an increase in fatigue. Some people tend to cry more frequently when they are depressed, while others experience fits of weeping. Many depressed people report being irritable much of the time.

Where Did the Positive Thoughts Go?

People who are depressed tend to experience thoughts that are both negative and hopeless. This hopelessness affects present thoughts, as well as thoughts about the future. As a result, it is difficult for a person who is depressed to enjoy a day's activities, and it is difficult for him or her to imagine a future that is bright and full of possibilities.

Those who are depressed also tend to find that they are anxious, and they experience dread that is out of proportion with actual events. As an example, a depressed person might experience extreme anxiety about doing something that he or she has always liked, such as attending a family picnic. Prior to the depression, attending such a social function would be regarded as an enjoyable way to spend time. Normally, then, this situation would not cause much anxiety at all. But to someone who is depressed, such a situation could evoke feelings of anxiety and even dread—so much so that he or she might decide to avoid the situation altogether and stay home. Simple events or tasks can seem threatening to the person who is depressed—even when there is little logical reason for this to be the case.

Someone who suffers from depression often has difficulty concentrating and making decisions. He or she may also experience feelings of guilt, self-loathing, and worthlessness. People who suffer from depression often find that they are preoccupied with thoughts of death and suicide—or even actually attempt to kill themselves.

The Body

Depression is not just a mental illness; it affects the body as well. If a parent is depressed, you may have noticed that he or she has experienced disruptions in normal eating and sleeping patterns. Many people who are depressed experience a loss of appetite, which can lead to weight loss. Other people may experience spurts of overeating. One's sleep can be affected, too. Some people suffering from depression are unable to sleep at all, while others wake up very early in the morning. Some depressed people may sleep many more hours than usual. Recent studies have shown that people who are depressed tend to get less "deep" sleep than those who are not suffering from depression. Deep sleep is the most restorative phase of sleep—which may explain why someone who is depressed may spend long hours sleeping, but will still feel exhausted when he or she is awake.

Other common symptoms of depression include a lack of interest in sex, an increase in headaches or stomachaches, and complaints of physical pain that affect other parts of the body.

Behavior

You might notice signs of depression in a parent's behavior. He or she might complain about having difficulty at work. Or, perhaps your parent finds that it takes great effort to accomplish simple tasks at home such as washing, dressing, and eating. Your parent may act restless, agitated, or jittery; experience slowed thoughts, movements, and speech; walk with a stooped and shuffling gait; or he or she may suddenly become extremely dependent on others.

It is important to note that not every depressed person will experience every one of these symptoms. Some people experience a few of these symptoms, while others may experience many or all of them. Also, the severity of symptoms varies with each individual. Your parent might be suffering from depression, but may not experience many outward symptoms. Your parent might act happier than he or she actually feels. Or your parent might have very strong outward symptoms—looking and acting sad all the time, and constantly talking about how depressed he or she feels.

Causes of Depression

For some people, the symptoms of depression seem to have no known cause, and they may persist even in the face of joyful events. People who are depressed often lack the energy to reach out for help, or they may feel so despondent that they believe any attempt to relieve their suffering will be futile. Not only do the symptoms of a depressed person vary, but the manifestations of these symptoms—and how each person handles his or her depression—vary as well.

Although what exactly is responsible for depression has not been isolated, most mental health professionals agree that a number of factors—both biochemical and psychological—work together to trigger depression. As with other mental illnesses, some people are more vulnerable to depression due to their genetic makeup. What this means is that a person may be born with a predisposition for depression. If depression runs in your family, you may be more at risk. Keep in mind, however, that just because a parent suffers from depression or just because it runs in your family does not mean that you are going to suffer from the disease as well.

Malfunctioning Neurotransmitters

Depression has been linked to the improper functioning of certain neurotransmitters in the brain. Neurotransmitters are chemical messengers that transmit electrical signals from one nerve cell to another. They control behavior, thoughts, and feelings. Studies have shown that people with depression have a deficit of two particular neurotransmitters, serotonin and norepinephrine. Other imbalances may involve a neurotransmitter called dopamine, as well as endocrine abnormalities. The endocrine system controls the production and functioning of the body's hormones.

Stress

Stress may also play a role in triggering depression. Any major life event—whether it is divorce or an illness, or an event considered to be positive, such as marriage or a new job—can bring on depression. Other factors that have been linked to depression are a lack of social support, feelings of isolation, and the feeling or belief that one is helpless.

Treatments for Depression

There are many effective treatments available for depression. Most people who are depressed can start to feel better in as little as three weeks after beginning a treatment plan. The different treatment options include medication, psychotherapy, and electroconvulsive therapy (ECT). The treatment plan may differ from person to person; for example, one person may require only medication, while another may require both medication and psychotherapy.

Antidepressants

Medicines used to treat depression are called antidepressants. There are many types, or classes, of antidepressants, and each works in a slightly different way. In general, antidepressants work by helping to fix the chemical imbalances in the brain that are often found in people with depression. There are other medications available for treating depression; one of these is benzodiazepine, which is a minor tranquilizer. This medication is effective in treating anxiety that may accompany depression, and it can also help a depressed person sleep better.

Psychotherapy

Psychotherapy is another effective treatment for depression. The most common type of psychotherapy involves speaking with a health-care professional about past experiences, relationships, thoughts, and feelings. This can be an effective and helpful way of learning new behaviors and coping strategies to deal with depression. Those undergoing psychotherapy can learn to think more positively and to take control of situations they would otherwise feel helpless in.

Psychotherapy used in the treatment of depression often lasts about six months, and is generally combined with the use of antidepressant medication.

Electroconvulsive Therapy

Electroconvulsive therapy (ECT) is another therapy that is used to fight depression. ECT is often used after medications and psychotherapy have not been successful. It is a safe and painless procedure where the patient receives mild electrical stimulation of the brain. ECT is usually administered two to three times each week for two to four weeks.

Coping with a Depressed Parent

If you suspect that your parent is depressed, talk to a trusted adult. You cannot be expected to look after your parent or to help find treatment for your parent—but another adult can. If you are the only family member living with your depressed parent, you might feel isolated. If this is the case, try to reach out to those around you; even if you do not have a large family, you can still discuss your parent's illness with a trusted adult or relative. Perhaps your teacher, principal, or guidance counselor can help. Maybe a friend can offer the emotional support you need. You can also seek the advice of a medical professional. The important thing to remember is that you are not alone, and you cannot and should not deal with this on your own.

Sometimes, families affected by depression can become isolated. Depression is a difficult thing for many people to talk about, and a lot of families try to cope as a family unit without asking for help or support from others. This isolation can cause added stress. Also, many people are unwilling to discuss their families' problems, for fear of breaching a certain kind of family loyalty.

Seek Help Early On

As previously mentioned, very few people snap out of depression. Most often, it is not a temporary state, but a more permanent one that requires assistance and treatment in order to be cured. Recent studies have shown that even if depression does go away on its own, it is likely to recur. Because of this, it makes sense to get help as early as possible in the course of a depression, both to alleviate pain and to lessen the chances that the depression will come back. Clinical studies have shown that treatment tends to be more successful the earlier it is begun.

What are some other signs that will indicate that it is time to seek help? Most experts agree that depression should be probably be treated when it causes prolonged difficulties with social and work activities and day-to-day functioning. However, you can also seek help from an adult when your parent's distress becomes severe. Your parent might be good at hiding the depression or acting like everything is fine. Despite this, you may have picked up on your parent's depression, or your parent may have told you that he or she is not feeling happy or is in need of help. It is important to listen to your parent, even if he or she was acting fine the day before, and then go to another adult for help.

Resisting Treatment

After seeking help from a trusted adult, you may discover that your parent is resistant to treatment. This is normal; many people who are depressed are unable to acknowledge that they have a problem. It is very common for a person to deny that he or she is in pain or is suffering. Also, it can be really frightening to begin dealing with a professional—many people think that the fact that they need to see a psychologist or psychiatrist (or other specialist) indicates that they are dealing with something beyond their control. This can be a terrifying realization to come to terms with. If your parent denies that he or she has a problem or is feeling differently, try not to worry too much and just give it some time. Eventually, your parent will come around and will be on the path to getting some help.

Bipolar Disorder

Jonas's Mother: Extreme Mood Swings

"My mother was always a bit on the moody side," says Jonas. "But it wasn't anything major, and didn't really affect anyone in our family. We thought of it more as a part of her personality than as something that was really wrong with her."

When Jonas was in ninth grade, he noticed a big difference in his mother's behavior. "My mother would have these really dark periods where she'd sit around and mope. During these phases, she'd miss work a lot, and she was really forgetful. One, night she forgot to make us dinner—something she has done every night since I can remember. Overall, she was cranky and irritable, and she often complained about having terrible headaches that prevented her from doing chores around the house."

Still more troubling to Jonas and his family was the fact that in between these phases of depression, his mother's behavior was even more out of the ordinary. "She would have these enormous bursts of energy," says Jonas, "where she would be running around the house, talking really fast, and coming up with these crazy ideas.

"One afternoon when I came home from school, she started rambling on and on about how she was going to go on this huge bike trip across the country. She was talking as though she was an avid cyclist, but I knew that she had only ridden a bike a few times in her life. Another time, she was talking really excitedly about how she was going to start a catering business, and how she would be the master chef and would have at least thirty employees. She seemed to forget about her job as an advertising executive. It was as though she suspended reality in favor of these whimsical ideas that were never going to happen. It was very strange, particularly coming from a woman who ordinarily had so much common sense."

It didn't take long before Jonas, his siblings, and their father held a family meeting. Their first meeting was without their mother—they just wanted to express their concerns to each other and talk about what was happening. Jonas and his father went to the library and after much reading, they thought that they had identified the illness that Jonas's mother suffered from. Fortunately, when Jonas's father brought up the issue with his wife, she was very receptive to the possibility of seeking outside help. It was with the help of a psychiatrist that Jonas's mother was diagnosed: She had bipolar disorder.

In chapter 2, we discussed the symptoms, causes, and treatments of depression. What, then, is bipolar disorder (sometimes called manic depression)? People with bipolar disorder have extreme mood swings that alternate from depression to mania. In the depressed phase of bipolar disorder, the symptoms are the same as those in depression: The depressed patient has a depressed mood and shows signs of decreased interest, sleep and appetite changes, and a loss of energy, among other symptoms.

In the manic phase of bipolar disorder, the symptoms are almost completely opposite to those experienced in the depressed phase. When a person experiences mania, he or she goes through an emotional state of intense elation that is evidenced in hyperactivity, talkativeness, a sporadic flightiness of ideas, distractibility, impractical and grandiose plans, and spurts of purposeless activity. There have been reports of individuals who experience mania but not depression, although this condition is rare.

Changes in Speech and Behavior

How can you tell if someone is manic? For one thing, manic symptoms are present in speech. The manic person's comments are loud and incessant. They are full of puns and jokes, and they often rhyme. People with mania often interject comments about nearby objects and things that have captured their attention, and those interjections may have absolutely nothing to do with the conversation. A manic person's speech is very difficult to interpret, often shifting from topic to topic and making little sense.

Manic symptoms are also present in behavior. People in a manic phase are very active. This can cause the person to be annoyingly sociable and intrusive. A person in the manic phase may act as though he or she is constantly busy, even though it is clear that he or she has nothing of importance to do. If someone tries to curb this momentum and slow the individual down, he or she may quickly become angry or even enraged. A person in the manic phase tends to be in an exceedingly good mood, and nothing, not even a terrible tragedy, can change this mood.

Other Signs of Mania

Other signs that a person is going through the manic phase include the following:

- Not sleeping or not eating for days.
- Acting self-confident and expressing optimism even when the situation doesn't warrant it. Affected individuals may experience delusions of grandeur such as having connections with political figures or with God. Also, he or she may believe that the laws of nature do not apply to him or her.
- Beginning many projects at once without being able to complete them. Also, people in the manic phase can become highly distracted by insignificant details.
- Buying impulsively and excessively.
- Using poor judgment, such as driving recklessly or making unwise and hasty business investments.
- Engaging in promiscuous or unusual sexual behavior. Becoming impatient, irritable, agitated, volatile, violent, and even psychotic if someone tries to slow them down. Some individuals with bipolar disorder are sent to prison because their acting-out behavior has led them to break the law.

As a further illustration of the mood swings a person with bipolar disorder may experience, compare the features of a depressive episode with a manic episode. As you can see, the features of each episode are nearly diametrically opposed.

Features of a Depressive Episode

- Persistent sad, anxious, or empty mood
- Feeling helpless, guilty, or worthless
- Hopeless or pessimistic feelings
- Loss of pleasure in usual activities
- Decreased energy
- Loss of memory or concentration
- Irritability or restlessness
- Sleep disturbances
- Loss of or increase in appetite
- Persistent thoughts of death

Features of a Manic Episode

- Extreme irritability and distractibility
- Excessive "high" or euphoric feelings

- Sustained periods of unusual, even bizarre, behavior with significant risk-taking
- Increased energy, increased activity, and rapid talking and thinking; agitation
- Decreased sleep
- Poor judgment
- Increased sex drive
- Substance abuse
- Provocative or obnoxious behavior
- Denial of a problem

As with other mental illnesses, people experience bipolar disorder in different ways. Some people experience full blown mania, in which the individual experiences many of the symptoms listed above. Other patients have what is called hypomania, where the mania feels less pronounced, and the symptoms aren't quite as exaggerated. Mania often comes on suddenly, over the period of a day or two. Untreated episodes may last from a few days to several months. These symptoms are often severe enough to cause serious impairment in social and occupational functioning.

Bipolar Disorder Versus Clinical Depression

Bipolar disorder occurs less often than clinical depression—clinical depression affects approximately 15 million Americans, while bipolar disorder affects about 2.2 million Americans.

Unlike depression, which can strike at any time, bipolar disorder usually begins during adolescence and early adulthood. The average onset age of bipolar disorder is thirty, and it occurs equally often in men and women. Bipolar disorder tends to recur, meaning that the cycle of depression and mania is usually experienced more than just once.

The Early Stages of Bipolar Disorder

A person at the beginning of a manic phase may feel powerful, full of energy, giddy with excitement, bubbly, and elated. In other words, the beginning phase of mania can feel really great to the person experiencing it. But these phases can turn into much more intense and active periods where life seems to spin out of control. These manic episodes are nearly always followed by a deep depression. Sometimes this occurs immediately, or a few months can pass before the depression begins. Then there may be a long interval during which the person behaves normally. Severely affected people may have what is called rapid cycling, in which the mood swings occur almost continuously.

An early sign of bipolar disorder may be hypomania—where the afflicted person shows a high level of energy, excessive moodiness or irritability, and impulsive or reckless behavior. Hypomania may feel good to the person who experiences it. Thus, even when family and friends learn to recognize the mood swings, the individual will often deny that anything is wrong. In its early stages, bipolar disorder may masquerade as a problem other than mental illness, such as alcohol or drug abuse or poor school/work performance. If left untreated, bipolar disorder tends to worsen, and the person experiences episodes of full-fledged mania and clinical depression.

Causes of Bipolar Disorder

To date, the cause of bipolar disorder is unknown. We do know, however, that bipolar disorder tends to run in families, and there is strong evidence that it is inherited. It has been found that between 80 and 90 percent of people who are afflicted with this illness have relatives with some type of depression. But people with a genetic predisposition—that is, people who are more likely to have the disease because of a genetic link—do not always develop the illness. In other words, even though your parent or family member might suffer from bipolar disorder, this does not mean that you will suffer from it as well. As with other mental illnesses, environmental factors play a role in determining the onset of the disease.

Because many people who suffer from bipolar disorder respond to medication that alters brain chemistry, it seems likely that this illness is caused, at least in part, by an imbalance of the neurotransmitters in the brain. Also, as with other mental illnesses, it appears that bipolar disorder is partly caused by certain abnormalities in the brain. Studies have found higher levels of stress hormones in people with bipolar disorder. Also, a specific area in the prefrontal cortex of the brain is smaller in people with bipolar disorder than in people without the disease.

Treatment of Bipolar Disorder

Thanks to new treatments, most sufferers of bipolar disorder can lead normal lives. A person with bipolar disorder can undergo psychological treatment in which the therapist helps the patient recognize the onset of a manic episode and take corrective action. A psychologist can provide your parent, you, and your family with education about the illness, as well as support and help with coping techniques. A psychologist can also help monitor the symptoms of bipolar disorder, as well as encourage your parent to continue with medical treatment. A psychologist is a mental health professional who works with individuals, families, and/or children. A psychiatrist is a mental health professional who is also a medical doctor and is therefore permitted to prescribe medications.

Get Help from a Psychiatrist

In addition, a patient with bipolar disorder should be under the care of a psychiatrist skilled in diagnosis and treatment of the disorder. The psychiatrist can monitor the medication that is usually required to help treat the disorder and control the mood swings. One medication, lithium, is often used to control mania. It also helps prevent the recurrence of both manic and depressive episodes of the disease. Other drugs, such as mood-stabilizing anticonvulsants called carbamazepine and valproate, have also been found useful in treating this illness. Often these medications are combined with lithium in order to have a maximum effect.

Charting Moods Can Be Helpful

Some health care professionals find it helpful to construct a chart of mood symptoms, medications, and life events in order to figure out how best to treat the illness, and to figure out which medications and therapy are most effective for each individual patient. Also, because bipolar disorder is recurrent, long-term preventive treatment is highly recommended.

Hospital Commitment

To ensure proper treatment and personal safety, commitment to a hospital may be necessary for a person in a severe episode of bipolar disorder. Hospital commitment, in which the patient is placed in the hospital against his/her will, is sometimes necessary with bipolar disorder because of the effects of the manic episodes. In other words, when the person is "high," he or she may engage in activities that are self-destructive or that may harm others. In these situations, the patient cannot understand the need for hospitalization because his or her judgment has been affected by the illness.

Dealing with a Parent Who Has Bipolar Disorder

As with other mental illnesses, bipolar disorder also creates problems for spouses, family members, friends, and employers. Family members of people with manic depression may have to cope with serious behavioral problems (such as wild spending sprees) and the lasting consequences of these behaviors.

If you suspect that your parent has bipolar disorder, talk to a trusted adult about the problem. He or she should be able to figure out what course of action to take. Keep in mind that it may take time to discover the best treatment regimen for an individual. It is very important—for your parent and for your entire family—to work with a psychologist and physician to develop the most appropriate treatment plan. In addition to treatment, self-help groups can benefit your parent, your family, and you. National Depressive and Manic-Depressive Association (NDMDA) and National Alliance for the Mentally Ill (NAMI) sponsor such groups; see the back of this book for more information.

4 Psychosis and Schizophrenia

Like depression, psychosis is a term many of us use in ordinary speech. When someone is acting silly or out of the ordinary, we may describe his or her behavior as being psychotic. However, the term has quite a different meaning to psychiatrists and mental health professionals. A person with psychosis has an impairment of thinking or mood in which his or her interpretation of reality and of daily events is severely abnormal.

Psychosis can be experienced with a variety of illnesses, such as schizophrenia, depression, and bipolar disorder. People with brain damage or who are under the influence of alcohol and drugs can also experience psychotic episodes. While psychological factors contribute to psychosis, there is substantial evidence that there are chemical abnormalities in the brains of people with this problem. To put it simply, psychosis is the ultimate result of a disordered brain.

Signs of Psychosis

Whatever the cause or nature of their problems, psychotic people often exhibit one or more of the following characteristics of the disease:

Disordered Thinking

People with disordered thinking suffer from delusions. In other words, they have false beliefs that have no basis in reality and that are not logical. An example of a delusion is when a person is convinced that there is a world conspiracy to "get them." Another example of a delusion is thinking that, two years ago, someone tried to slip poison into his or her drink—when, in fact, no such event occurred.

Disorders of Perception

From time to time, we all misinterpret our senses. Many of us (who do not suffer from psychosis) have experienced the following scenario: You watch a scary movie, and after the movie is over, you find that your senses are heightened. You might, for example, hear leaves falling outside your house, but you automatically think that there is someone walking around outside your house. This is a normal reaction and is not considered a psychiatric disorder. However, what is abnormal is a hallucination, in which a person thinks that something exists, but it is not really there. In this case, there is no confusion of the senses—in other words, there is no real reason for the person to think that a person or thing is there. As an example, a person might claim to hear music, when in reality, there is nothing there to produce the sound.

Language Disorders

We all know people who don't seem to make sense, or who continually interject boring stories into a conversation. These people may be annoying, but they are not considered psychotic. With a psychotic person, his or her communication is so distorted that he or she may be incapable of answering a question directly, or of sticking to any one topic. Someone who is psychotic might stop talking in mid-sentence and abruptly fall silent, only to resume talking a few moments later, completely unaware that there has been a disruption.

Disturbance of Affect

Many people with psychosis show emotions that are not consistent with what they are thinking. For example, a psychotic person might laugh when talking about death. Also, a psychotic person's emotions can fluctuate more rapidly than normal. As an example, a person with psychosis might laugh, cry, and show rage all within a few minutes. Other psychotic people may be consistently apathetic and dull.

As previously mentioned, psychosis can be seen in people with a variety of illnesses, and even with substance abuse. Those with schizophrenia, depression, bipolar disorder, and brain damage can experience psychotic episodes. Any of the psychotic symptoms may be caused by a physical abnormality or disturbance in the brain. In other words, a person may show psychotic symptoms after suffering brain damage, a tumor, an infection, epilepsy, hemorrhage, or exposure to toxins. In these cases, there will be medical evidence or clues from a physical examination that would explain the damage to the brain. Thus, the treatment of the psychosis depends on what brought on the psychosis.

Schizophrenia

Our understanding of the origins of schizophrenia—a disease that is characterized by disordered thinking, hallucinations, delusions, and a tendency to withdraw from reality—has come a long way, even in the last decade. Many years ago, people believed that faulty parenting was the cause of schizophrenia. Now, however, there is evidence that schizophrenia may be caused by a combination of defects that occur early in the brain's development as a result of genetic vulnerability and environmental triggers.

Schizophrenia is the most complex and puzzling of all mental illnesses. It is also the most debilitating. It affects about 1 percent of the population, and afflicts men and women equally. Each year, about 100,000 new cases of schizophrenia are diagnosed in the United States. Because of its early onset—in the late teens or early adulthood—and the possibility of lifelong disability, schizophrenia's effect on families can be catastrophic.

Many people think that schizophrenia means having a split personality or multiple personalities, where a person takes on more that one identity. However, this is not true. Rather, schizophrenia is a brain disease that can affect nearly every aspect of an individual's functioning. Schizophrenia is incredibly disabling and affects the senses and thinking. As with other mental illnesses, schizophrenia can manifest itself in different ways. For example, some sufferers of schizophrenia become quiet, anxious, and withdrawn. Others, however, can become very aggressive and quite outspoken in their speech and behavior.

People in an acute phase of schizophrenia are said to be psychotic, a state described at the beginning of this chapter. When a schizophrenic patient is psychotic, it means that he or she is out of touch with reality. It also means that he or she may be unable to separate real experiences from unreal ones. Some schizophrenics may have only one psychotic episode in a lifetime, while others have many, but are still able to lead relatively normal lives during the interim periods. Unfortunately, for some, schizophrenia is a chronic disorder that affects them for life.

Saul's Battle with Schizophrenia

When Saul was eighteen, he was beginning to show signs of schizophrenia. Saul's parents were both doctors—his mother was a psychiatrist, and his father was a pediatrician—and they began to recognize in Saul the symptoms of schizophrenia.

At first, Saul withdrew from his friends and family, choosing instead to be on his own. His parents didn't think too much of that—after all, he was at an age when he was trying to be more independent. But he displayed other symptoms shortly after the withdrawal started. His thoughts and language were jumbled and often made little sense.

"One night I woke up to Saul screaming from his room," Saul's mother recalls. "I ran across the hall to find Saul yelling at an 'intruder'—only there wasn't anyone there. When Saul finally calmed down, it was clear that he was utterly convinced someone was there. I was hoping that he was confused from a dream he was having, and that he would snap out of

it, but no such luck. When I asked him about the incident the next morning, he was able to describe in vivid detail what the intruder looked like, what he said, and so on."

"There were many similar incidents to this one," says Saul's father. "Because of my medical background, I was able to recognize some of his symptoms. Of course, as a father I was a little in denial, both of us were," he says, referring to Saul's mother. "We just didn't want to believe that our son was afflicted with mental illness. I researched our family tree, only to discover that my family has a history of mental illness. While some of my ancestors were not actually diagnosed, they were often described as being 'mad' or eccentric." In fact, Saul's great grandfather had been committed to a mental institution.

Saul's sister recalls coming home from college and seeing a very different brother than the one she had left behind a few months earlier. "There wasn't the same connection between us anymore," she admits. "I could sense it the second I walked in the door. Saul was watching television when I came in, and he barely looked up when I entered the room. In the past, Saul would have jumped out of his chair to give me a big hug. When I tried to talk to him, he just rambled on and on, and he wasn't making any sense."

Those suffering from schizophrenia may experience a variety of symptoms. Some of these symptoms, which are similar to the signs of psychosis, include the following:

Inability to Think Straight

The schizophrenic's thoughts may come in rapid-fire succession without logical sequence. As a result, his or her sentences may be fragmented or jumbled.

Auditory or Visual Hallucinations

Auditory hallucinations are hallucinations that are heard. In other words, a schizophrenic with auditory hallucinations hears voices in his or her head—voices telling him or her what to do or what not to do, warning him or her of danger, or insulting the person who is hearing them. A person with visual hallucinations (in other words, hallucinations that can be seen) sees things that the rest of us do not.

False Beliefs

A schizophrenic may think that the radio is broadcasting his or her thoughts or that aliens are controlling his or her behavior. The beliefs may be grandiose, such as believing that he or she is God. These beliefs might also involve paranoia—believing that a present is a bomb, or that a drink is poisoned, for instance.

Inappropriate Emotions

Schizophrenics may laugh when they should be crying, cry when they should be laughing, or at times, show no emotions at all. For example, a schizophrenic may react to a grim situation with joyous laughter and shouting, as opposed to expressing the appropriate melancholy or more subdued behavior.

Emotional and Social Withdrawal

Schizophrenia may involve emotional and social withdrawal, a lack of motivation, and/or reduced verbal and emotional expressiveness. A schizophrenic may experience any of these behavioral states, and as you might imagine, these can seriously impair personal relationships.

Other Signs and Symptoms

There are many other symptoms of schizophrenia. One of these is catatonia, in which schizophrenics may grimace or adopt strange facial expressions. They may gesture repeatedly, using peculiar and sometimes complex sequences of finger, hand, and arm movements. Often, these movements seem to have a purpose, but it is hard for others to decode their intended meaning.

Some schizophrenics exhibit an unusual increase in their overall level of activity, including much excitement, wild flailing of the limbs, and a great expenditure of energy similar to that of mania. Some schizophrenics experience catatonic immobility, in which unusual postures are adopted and maintained for very long periods of time. For example, a patient may stand on one leg, with the other tucked up, and remain in this position all day. Catatonic patients may also have what is referred to as waxy flexibility—where another person can move the patient's limbs into strange positions that will then be maintained for long periods of time.

As with other mental illnesses, different patients may have different signs and symptoms of the disease. For example, one patient may have hallucinations and may experience a lack of emotions, while another patient might have disorganized speech and delusions.

Causes of Schizophrenia

What causes schizophrenia? At the beginning of this section, we mentioned that there is now evidence pointing to the fact that schizophrenia may be caused by a combination of defects that occur early in the brain's development as a result of a genetic vulnerability, as well as environmental triggers. But what does this mean? Let's talk about genetic vulnerability first.

Genetic vulnerability refers to the fact that someone may be predisposed—or more likely—to develop a disease than someone else. Keep in mind, however, that even though your parent has schizophrenia, this does not necessarily mean that you will also develop the disease. Recent studies have shown that certain brain abnormalities that lead to schizophrenia may be present at birth. Some research has found that people with schizophrenia are more likely than normal children to have lags and surges in development during infancy, as well as social adjustment and achievement problems as school-age children. Hence, although the most obvious symptoms do not become apparent until adolescence and early adulthood, schizophrenia is a disease that begins early in life.

Research has shown that schizophrenics' brains differ in many ways from the brains of people without the illness. These differences include the following:

The Cortex

The cortex is a major part of the brain's gray matter and is involved in sensing, moving, and thinking. Research has shown that the frontal lobes of the cortex do not become as active as they do in the brains of people without the disease.

Ventricles

We all have fluid-filled spaces in our brains, called ventricles; however, in schizophrenics, these ventricles are enlarged.

The Prefrontal Cortex

The prefrontal cortex is part of the frontal lobes located just over the eyes. This part of our brain is the seat of what is called the "working memory"—our ability to hold new bits of information and to interrelate them with what we already know, and to release the information we no longer need to hold onto. It allows us to understand spoken language, as well as accomplish tasks in which we must remember visual images that are no longer in view. People with schizophrenia experience a malfunction in this area. They have difficulty clearing their working memory of irrelevant information and keeping visual images in mind after they have disappeared from sight.

The Thalamus

The thalamus is a part of the brain that helps us filter, process, and relay input from our senses, emotions, and memory. A person with a defective thalamus—in other words, a thalamus that is not working properly—will likely be flooded with information and overwhelmed with stimuli. On average, schizophrenics have a smaller thalamus than does the rest of the population.

When you take all of this into consideration—that the brain has difficulty functioning normally because of several different defects—you can see why this condition would make it difficult for various parts of the brain to communicate with one another.

Causes of Brain Defects

What causes these defects in the brain? There are numerous prenatal (meaning before birth) possibilities. Studies have shown that the misfiring of neurons (brain cells) can occur around the fourth to sixth month of pregnancy. This stage is very important in the development of the brain, since this is when the brain is organizing itself and neurons are settling into their proper places within the brain. Also, at this time, the cortex is growing rapidly.

What might interfere with this process and development? For one thing, a dietary deficiency or severe malnutrition in the mother could cause interference. Also, an attack in influenza (commonly called the flu) or another viral infection in the pregnant mother could interfere with this process and cause these various defects in the brain.

Some research suggests that schizophrenia may have something to do with the exposure to toxins (such as alcohol or amphetamines) or radiation that could cause problems in the brain's development.

Oxygen deprivation is another possible cause. This can happen if the umbilical cord wraps around the neck of the fetus, or if the mother's placenta is torn or becomes compressed.

Another factor that seems to be involved in schizophrenia is dopamine, a neurotransmitter in the brain that regulates movement and influences mood and motivation. The brains of people with schizophrenia seem to have too much dopamine. So far, it is unclear how dopamine affects schizophrenia, although it is clear that it plays an important role in this disease.

Schizophrenia's Genetic Link

There is strong evidence that schizophrenia runs in families. Research shows that what is inherited is not the disease itself, but rather a predisposition for developing the disease. In other words, someone may be more likely to develop schizophrenia depending on his or her genetic makeup. If someone has a predisposition for developing schizophrenia, and he or she is also affected by the environment (such as experiencing low oxygen or a viral infection as a fetus), he or she may be at a greater risk for having a defect in brain development. Ultimately, this can lead to schizophrenia.

Nongenetic factors, such as being born during the winter and being born in an urban area, can also increase the relative risk of schizophrenia. It is possible that infections during childhood and other factors related to urban birth may play a part in causing schizophrenia.

Treatment of Schizophrenia

Unfortunately, there is no known cure for schizophrenia. However, there are a number of medications that can help reduce the illness's symptoms. Neuroleptics, which have been prescribed since the 1950s, have proven effective in suppressing hallucinations, delusions, and disorganized thinking. Before neuroleptics were discovered, schizophrenics were treated with physical restraint—thus, this was an important medical discovery.

Medications

Thorazine is one of the best known neuroleptics. It works by decreasing the amount and overactivity of dopamine in the brain. Unfortunately, neuroleptics are only successful for relieving the hallucinations, delusions, and disorganized thoughts associated with schizophrenia. They are not effective in relieving the other symptoms (also called the "negative symptoms" of schizophrenia), which include a lack of interest in activities and people, decreased motivation and self-care, and a reduced ability for communication and emotional expression. These symptoms—which often result in withdrawal and social isolation—can be extremely disabling.

Neuroleptics are not, however, the perfect medication for schizophrenics. As with all medications, patients respond differently to these drugs. For some schizophrenics, neuroleptics do not work on their symptoms at all. For others, they cause many side effects, such as muscle spasms, tremors, a stiff gait, slowed speech, and sexual dysfunction. The most serious side effect is tardive dyskinesia (TD), a dreadful condition that is sometimes irreversible.

A person with TD experiences repetitive involuntary movements, such as lip smacking, facial grimacing, and abnormal gestures. This condition develops later on in a treatment cycle, usually after a few years. Therefore, despite the obvious benefits of neuroleptics, these side effects often leave patients with a great deal of mental and physical impairment.

New Medications

New medications are being developed all of the time. Clozapine (also called Clozaril) is the first of this new class and it is effective for at least a third of those patients who have not responded to traditional medications. Clozapine has been proven to help many symptoms of schizophrenia with fewer side effects and with no risk of causing tardive dyskinesia. However, for 1 to 2 percent of patients, Clozapine can produce a life-threatening blood disorder, so patients using this medication must have their blood checked regularly.

It should also be noted that schizophrenia does not usually involve deterioration, nor does it tend to progress to dementia. In other words, the degree of impairment in a patient with schizophrenia is relatively stable after the initial adjustment period (which may take a number of years). After that point, it is even possible for cognitive function in a schizophrenic patient to improve.

Future Research of Schizophrenia

The success of Clozapine—a drug that provides great relief without terrible side effects—has led to much promise and hope in the search for new drugs to treat schizophrenia. Risperidone (also called Risperdal), which was introduced in 1996, is currently the most widely prescribed medication for schizophrenia in the nation. While Risperidone has similar effects to Clozapine with regard to symptoms (without the danger of developing the blood disorder), in many people, Risperidone is not quite as effective in treating schizophrenia's negative symptoms.

Other promising new medications include Olanzapine (also called Zyprexa), which may affect more areas of the brain than either Clozapine or Risperidone, while having fewer side effects.

The Option of Therapy for Schizophrenics

While medications are extremely important in the treatment of schizophrenia, therapy is also an important part of treatment. Many schizophrenics find that, with the help of medications, their psychotic personalities dissipate, and they are left feeling more "normal"—free of many of the schizophrenic symptoms they were experiencing. Patients often find it difficult to adjust to their new world, a world free of delusion and hallucinations. Because this adjustment can be difficult, it is important for the schizophrenic and his or her family to engage in therapy to help ease the transition.

Depression and suicide are serious threats, especially when schizophrenic patients realize that they have lost so many years of their lives. Also, because the illness reaches its full form during adolescence and early adulthood, many patients find that they have missed important developmental and educational milestones. Their lives have been so occupied by their illness, and dealing with their illness, that they realize they have never learned to do things that healthy people take for granted.

Finding and keeping a job, making and keeping friends, and even going to school are uncharted territories for the schizophrenic. Because of this, readjusting to a more normal life is a hard thing to do, and therapy can help ease the transition.

Coping with a Schizophrenic Parent

If you suspect that your parent has schizophrenia, tell a trusted adult who will be able to assess the situation and take appropriate action. You will probably find it helpful to go to the library and do some research on your own. Also, talking with a medical professional can help you learn more about the illness.

Many schizophrenics find group counseling with peers to be particularly helpful in terms of offering support and helping them to readjust their social lives. Therapy, whether group or individual, can help schizophrenics reconstruct their personalities and regain self-esteem. Family therapy is also important; if you are the offspring of a schizophrenic patient, your doctor might suggest this as a possibility.

Panic Disorder

5

We all feel anxious from time to time. You might experience anxiety when you are about to start a new class or activity, when you fight with a friend, or when you are about to give a presentation in front of a large group of people. A little bit of anxiety is normal, and can even have positive effects: It can keep you alert and can provide you with extra energy.

But for people with anxiety disorders, the anxiety grows and grows until the person is not able to function properly. An anxiety disorder isn't just an excess of nerves; it is a disease, and it is, in fact, the most common of all mental illnesses. There are several types of anxiety disorders, each of which has its own set of symptoms. The most common anxiety disorders are panic disorder, phobias, and obsessive-compulsive disorder (OCD).

Panic Disorders and Phobias

Sufferers of panic disorder are subject to attacks of panic for no real cause. People with panic disorder have feelings of terror that strike suddenly, repeatedly, and without warning. They can't predict when an attack will occur, and they may develop intense anxiety between episodes, worrying when and where the next one will strike. In between attacks, there is a persistent, lingering fear that another attack could come at any minute. The typical symptoms of anxiety disorders include:

- Dizziness, sweating, cold flashes, shakiness, trembling, and/or faintness
- Nausea or abdominal distress
- Tightness in the chest, racing or pounding heartbeat
- Difficulty breathing, shortness of breath, and/or choking
- Terror; a sense that something horrible is about to occur and that you are powerless to prevent it
- Fear of losing control and of doing something you might think is embarrassing
- Fear of dying

Panic attacks can occur at any time, even during sleep. While most attacks average a couple of minutes, occasionally they can go on for as long as ten minutes. In rare cases, they may last an hour or more.

Phobias are often the result of panic attacks. People who suffer a panic attack often change their behavior to prevent another one. For example, if you experience a panic attack while driving, you might choose to avoid driving in the future, with the hope of preventing another attack. It is for this reason that many people who suffer from panic attacks are eventually afraid to leave the house. They then develop agoraphobia, which is when the afflicted person is afraid of open spaces and becomes homebound.

Consider the case of Arden's mother, Jane, who developed a fear of elevators after having her first panic attack on one.

Arden's Mother's Panic Attack

Jane was an outgoing forty-five-year-old who loved to be active and to be around people. She had many friends and was constantly meeting people through her love of outdoor activities and sports. She belonged to a skydiving club, was the captain of her neighborhood summer soccer league, and frequently went on whitewater rafting excursions in Colorado.

"My mother was afraid of nothing," says Arden, Jane's fifteen-year-old daughter. "She was always up for a challenge, and she was always learning new sports and participating in different activities. She had more energy than our whole family put together!"

Jane and Arden decided to go on a trip to New York City together. "We were having a great time," says Jane. "We got up really early in the morning and saw all the touristy things. On our last night, we decided to go to the top of the Empire State Building. We had heard that the view of the city was spectacular, and we were really looking forward to it."

Once they got to the top, however, it was a different story. "Right before my mother was about to step out onto the outside deck, she stopped walking," says Arden. "I was so excited to be there that I barely noticed. I went outside and took in the view, and it was then that I realized that she was gone. I retraced my steps, and when I found her—well, it was a bit of a shock." Arden ran into her mother by the elevator bank; Jane was leaning against a wall, looking pale and out of breath. "What I remember most," says Arden, "is that my mom looked really, really frightened."

"It was a really strange, scary feeling," says Jane. "Everything was completely fine—until I stepped on the elevator. The elevator was really crowded, and all of a sudden I started to feel hot and sweaty. My heart began racing, and I felt as though I might collapse or have some sort of seizure or attack. I didn't know what was going on. When the elevator finally reached the top, I got out with everyone else, but I was so freaked out by the experience, I stayed behind and tried to catch my breath."

Panic disorder strikes at least 1.6 percent of the population and it is twice as common in women as in men. It can appear at any age—in children or in the elderly—but most often it begins in young adulthood. In fact, roughly half of all people who have panic disorder develop the condition before age twenty-five. Not everyone who experiences panic attacks will develop panic disorder, however. Many people have one attack and never experience another one.

Because people with anxiety disorders worry about having another attack, attempts to change their behavior in order to avoid attacks also becomes a part of this illness. People with anxiety disorders can become so affected by their illness that their lives become restricted; they find themselves unable to work, drive, go shopping, or even leave their homes. Or, they may be able to confront a feared situation only if accompanied by a spouse or another trusted person. Basically, they avoid any situation they fear would make them feel helpless if a panic attack were to occur.

People with panic disorder may also have irritable bowel syndrome, characterized by intermittent bouts of gastrointestinal cramps and diarrhea or constipation, or a relatively minor heart problem that is called mitral valve prolapse.

About 30 percent of people with panic disorder use alcohol, and 17 percent use drugs—such as cocaine and marijuana—in unsuccessful attempts to alleviate the anxiety and distress caused by their condition. Appropriate diagnosis and treatment of other disorders such as substance abuse or depression are important to successfully treat panic disorder. In addition, approximately 20 percent of people with panic disorder attempt suicide.

The Causes of Panic Disorder

What causes panic disorder? The exact cause of this disease is unknown. Possible causes include heredity, other biological factors, and stressful life events. Some professionals believe that panic disorder may be caused by an individual overreacting to the sweaty palms and racing heart that often appear as the first signs of anxiety. Whereas some people are able to dismiss these signs as simple annoyances, others aren't, and may even misinterpret them as being a part of a greater problem. For example, a person with sweaty palms and a racing heart could mistakenly attribute these symptoms to being part of larger problem, such as a heart attack.

The Role of Genetics

As with most mental illnesses, scientists have now learned that genetics, brain chemicals (neurotransmitters), and brain structures all seem to play a role in panic disorder. There are signs that this disease has genetic roots; in fact, higher rates of panic disorder have been found among both parents and siblings of those with the illness. Remember, however, that just because your parent or sibling has panic disorder does not mean that you will develop the disease.

The Amygdala

Another theory about what causes panic disorder has to do with what is called the amygdala, which is an almond-shaped region in the brain. The amygdala is involved in deciding whether a noise or a sight we experience is worthy of a fearful reaction. Usually, the amygdala makes a split-second determination and moves on to monitoring the next experience.

The theory in panic disorder, however, is that the amygdala responds powerfully to false alarms or becomes fixated on a stimulus—such as finding oneself on a high floor with no easy way down—and doesn't move on. Instead, it repeatedly tells the rest of the brain that there is something grave to fear, which causes it to release a deluge of neurotransmitters. This reaction can produce a rapid heartbeat, sweating, and dizziness, among other symptoms.

Treatment of Panic Disorder

Fortunately, there are many available treatments for panic disorder. As a rule, panic disorder is thought to be a very treatable illness. For starters, studies have shown that proper treatment—a type of psychotherapy called cognitive-behavioral therapy, medications, or possibly a combination of the two—helps 70 to 90 percent of people with panic disorder. Significant improvement is usually seen within six to eight weeks. Relapses may occur, but they can often be effectively treated just like the initial episode.

Most research indicates that the most effective treatments for panic disorder involve drug therapy and cognitive-behavioral therapy. In drug therapy, the use of antidepressants (such as Prozac, Paxil, and Zoloft) have proven to be very useful. Antidepressants work to increase the levels of serotonin in the brain. Also, antianxiety medications have been proven to work in treating panic disorder. As with other mental illnesses, treatment often proceeds by trial and error. In other words, one patient may respond very well to Prozac; for another, Prozac may cause aggravating side effects, and Paxil may work better. Also, some people may respond very well to cognitive-behavioral therapy, while others might not respond to this type of treatment at all.

As previously mentioned, cognitive-behavioral therapy can be very useful in helping to overcome panic disorders. One technique in cognitive-behavioral therapy, called exposure therapy, can often help alleviate the phobias that may result from panic disorder. In exposure therapy, people are very slowly exposed to a fearful situation until they become desensitized to it. Let's look at Monita's father's experience with this type of therapy.

Overcoming a Fear of Snakes: Monita's Father

"Ever since I can remember, my father has been afraid of snakes," says Monita. "I can't recall him ever having had a bad experience with a snake, but my grandmother does. She says that when he was a young boy, he had his nose pressed up against the glass at a zoo. My grandmother was holding him, and apparently, the snake lurched toward the glass and opened his mouth wide—like he was going to hiss. I guess dad was scared by that. Over the next several weeks, according to my grandmother, my father had nightmares about snakes, and would wake up shaking or in tears. Eventually, though, his nightmares stopped, but his fear of snakes remained."

Although Monita's father's fear of snakes wasn't debilitating, and it didn't affect his life in any major way, he wanted to do something about it. "I hated that I had this fear for years," he says. "It felt so silly—after all, I'm a grown man! So I decided to see a therapist about it." His therapist worked out a plan. The first step was to go to a zoo and look at a snake from a distance. "It seems ridiculous, but even this first phase of treatment increased my anxiety and made me afraid," he says. "But my therapist talked me through it. We were standing about ten feet away from the snake, and my therapist taught me to deal with my anxiety, showing me that there was nothing to be scared of." Monita's dad and his therapist continued this routine, and slowly they worked their way closer to the glass. "To the casual observer, my progress might have seemed slow, but after about a month of therapy, I was still unable to get right up to the glass," he says. "But I felt great, and I was encouraged by my progress."

Eventually, Monita's father was able to walk right up to the snake and not feel any anxiety at all. He is still continuing treatment, however, because his goal is to be able to one day hold a snake with complete confidence. "Six months ago, that would have seemed like a complete impossibility," Monita's father says. "But I know that it will happen, and I can't wait."

Cognitive-behavioral approaches teach patients how to view panic situations differently. They demonstrate ways to reduce anxiety, using breathing exercises or other techniques.

Coping with Panic Disorder

Many people with panic disorder are aware that there is a problem, and are embarrassed by their behavior. For example, a person who has a panic attack in an elevator, and later develops a phobia about the elevator, knows that this is an irrational fear. But panic attacks can be so terrifying that the person who suffers from them feels that he or she has no choice in the matter: There is nothing to do but avoid situations where panic attacks are likely to occur.

Your Role

As you read in the treatment section, there are many effective treatments for panic disorder. You may see things that others do not—for example, your parent's friends or coworkers might not realize that there is a problem at all. But as the son or daughter of a mentally ill parent, you are in the unique position of being around your parent for much of the time. Thus, you might be able to recognize that there is a problem, and you can bring this to the attention of an adult you feel comfortable confiding in. You can also offer to accompany your parent to a therapist. Remember, even a seemingly small gesture can go a long way toward helping someone.

Obsessive-Compulsive Disorder

We all have little quirks and habits that we're sure we'd be better off without. You might have experienced a scenario similar to the following: You leave your house, but then go back in to make sure that you have turned off all the lights and the stove. Or, perhaps you have a ritual when you get ready in the morning, and you believe that if you forget a step in that ritual—such as not putting your socks on before your pants or brushing your teeth after taking a shower instead of doing so before—the rest of your day will be a bad one.

While these thoughts or behaviors seem silly, they don't tend to pose much of a disruption to our everyday lives. However, in obsessive-compulsive disorder, or OCD (as it is most commonly called), these behaviors and thoughts spin out of control so much that they prevent a person from living a normal life.

What Obsessive-Compulsive Means

What does the term "obsessive-compulsive" mean? First, let's start with the term "obsession." An obsession is an intrusive, unwelcome, and distressing thought or mental image. Obsessive thoughts can be annoying; the person experiencing such a thought will long for it to go away, but when it doesn't and instead continues to spin around and around in one's head, this situation can lead to excessive anxiety and distress. Obsessive thoughts do not fade; on the contrary, they keep intruding into your thoughts.

A compulsion (the other half of the term "obsessive-compulsive") is a behavior that people with OCD perform in an attempt to get rid of the fears and anxieties caused by their obsessions. In other words, if a person believes that washing their hands fifty times a day will prevent a death in their family, the act of washing their hands is the compulsion.

Performing Rituals in Order to "Prevent" Catastrophes

People with OCD often engage in bizarre and self-destructive behavior that will, they believe, help prevent a major catastrophe. However, there is no realistic connection between the behaviors and the catastrophes they fear. As an example, a person with OCD might shower thirty times a day to "ensure" that the day will go well.

An OCD sufferer might go to great lengths to avoid writing or speaking a certain number so that he or she can "prevent" an illness. Rationally, of course, these actions aren't linked to the catastrophes; it is simply not possible that taking a shower thirty times a day will ensure that a day will run smoothly.

Current estimates show that approximately five million Americans (or one in fifty) are afflicted with OCD. The illness affects all age groups.

Common Symptoms of OCD

There are numerous symptoms of OCD. To give you an idea of the extent of the beliefs and behaviors involved, the following are some of the most common obsessions and compulsions.

Obsessions About Dirt and Contamination

- Unfounded fears of contracting a dreadful illness
- Excessive concerns about dirt, germs, and environmental contaminants (such as household cleaners)
- Feelings of revulsion and disgust about bodily waste and secretions
- Obsessions about one's body
- Abnormal concerns about sticky substances or other residues

Obsessive Need for Order or Symmetry

- An overwhelming need to align objects
- Abnormal concerns about the neatness of one's personal appearance or one's environment

Obsessions About Hoarding or Saving

- Stashing away useless trash, such as old newspapers or items rescued from trash cans

- The inability to discard anything because it may be needed at some time; a fear of losing or discarding something by mistake

Obsessions with Sexual Content

- Repeated sexual thoughts that are viewed by others as being inappropriate and unacceptable

Repetitive Rituals

- Repeating routine activities for no logical reason

- Repeating questions over and over

- Rereading or rewriting words or phrases

There are many other symptoms of obsessive-compulsive disorder, such as religious obsessions and obsessions with aggressive content (such as the fear of acting out a violent thought). Likewise, there are many common symptoms of compulsions. These include:

Cleaning and Washing Compulsions

- Excessive, ritualized hand washing, showering, bathing, or toothbrushing

- The unshakable feeling that household items, such as dishes, are contaminated or cannot be washed enough to be really clean

Compulsions About Having Things "Just Right"

- The need for symmetry and total order in one's environment. For example, the need to line up canned goods in the pantry in alphabetical order, to hang clothes in exactly the same spot in the closet every day, or to wear certain clothes only on certain days

- The need to keep doing something until one gets it "just right"

Hoarding or Collecting Compulsions

- Minutely inspecting household trash in case a "valuable" item has been thrown out

- Accumulating useless objects

Checking Compulsions

- Repeatedly checking to see if a door is locked or if an appliance is turned off

- Checking and rechecking mistakes, such as when balancing a checkbook

- Repeatedly checking oneself and one's body for signs of a catastrophic disease

There are many more compulsive behaviors that are not listed here. Some of these include the need to touch, tap, or rub certain objects repeatedly; counting compulsions, such as counting tiles in the floor or billboards on a highway; and mental rituals, such as reciting silent prayers in an effort to make a bad thought go away.

Consider the following cases of Hector, Lara, and Edwin, who all suffer from OCD, but in different forms.

Three Examples of People Suffering From OCD

Joey's father, Hector, developed an obsession with germs.

> *"I washed my hands frequently, but that wasn't even the half of it," he says. Hector's daily life consisted of constantly dusting, cleaning, and scrubbing surfaces that he had cleaned just minutes before. "Nothing could be clean enough," says Hector. "I would clean my bathroom incessantly—so much so that I ended up taking the finish off my cabinets. But even that didn't stop me. It was as though something in my brain was telling me over and over again that I needed to keep cleaning." As you might imagine, Hector's behavior began to interfere with his life. "I stopped going out so that I would be able to devote all of my energy to cleaning," he says.*

Lily's mother, Lara, had a different problem. She had what is called a "checking compulsion," where she always had to check on things. For example, she was never convinced that the door to her apartment was locked and that her coffee machine was unplugged.

"I would check my coffee maker and then I'd leave the apartment," says Lara. "But the furthest I'd ever get was down the hall. Then I would go back to my apartment to make sure it was locked. And then I'd have to unlock the door and check to make sure that the coffee maker was unplugged. It was an awful, vicious cycle, and one that I'd repeat many times each day to no avail. Even if I managed to actually leave my apartment, I would sit at work and worry about whether or not the coffee machine was plugged in."

Elizabeth's father, Edwin, believed that by washing his hands fifty times a day, he could prevent anything bad from happening to his family.

"I'm not sure where this belief came from," Edwin explains. "But I do know that it severely affected my life. I washed my hands so often that they were always dry, and sometimes they even bled." Edwin was embarrassed about his compulsion, but he lived alone, so many people did not know about it. "I limited my hand washing to my apartment," Edwin says. "I wouldn't wash my hands excessively at work or in public."

But Edwin got a wake-up call when a friend from out of town stayed with him. "I was so embarrassed, but I didn't have a choice," Edwin says. "It wasn't like I had an option just to not wash my hands. I simply had to." Edwin's friend tried to talk to Edwin about the problem, and he made Edwin promise to seek treatment. The friend also told Elizabeth what was going on with her father.

Getting "Stuck"

One of the latest theories about obsessive-compulsive disorder is that it occurs when the brain gets "stuck." A person with this disorder may wash his or her hands, and then the brain says: "Wash your hands again." The afflicted person will do so, even though there is no reason to. Unfortunately, once people give in to these irresistible urges, their compulsions become even stronger. In other words, if a person gives in to his or her obsessions and compulsions, the brain gets "worse," and the person will feel compelled to do the behavior more often. If he or she doesn't give in, the brain becomes unstuck or "better," and the obsession or compulsion decreases.

It should be noted that people with OCD do not enjoy their repetitive behaviors. One of the horrifying aspects of OCD is that sufferers are all too aware of the illogical nature of their compulsions. They are completely aware of how inappropriate their behavior is and often feel ashamed and embarrassed by it.

Causes of OCD

What causes obsessive-compulsive disorder? It is a neurological problem, meaning that the brain does not work properly. There is some scientific evidence that obsessive-compulsive disorder is related to a genetic predisposition that causes people to develop the illness.

Researchers are looking closely at the role that serotonin, a neurotransmitter in the brain, plays in OCD. Antidepressant medications, which increase the levels of serotonin, have produced considerable improvement in people with OCD, so it seems likely that serotonin is involved. Also, researchers have discovered that levels of other brain chemicals are significantly higher in people with OCD.

There is also some evidence that shows that infections such as strep throat may trigger an autoimmune response in children who are genetically vulnerable for this illness. Such infections can cause or worsen a sudden case of childhood OCD.

Treatments of OCD

Different treatments work for different people.

Habituation

Recent studies have shown that it can be possible to change the chemistry of your brain by using cognitive-behavioral therapy. The focus of such therapy is a process called "habituation," during which the patient learns to confront his or her fears and reduce his or her anxiety without performing the rituals he or she normally performs. Gradually, the person exposes himself or herself to situations that cause anxiety, but refrains from performing the rituals that usually relieve the anxiety.

For example, let's say that a patient is particularly concerned with germs and contamination. Part of the therapy of this individual would be to teach him or her to deal with a germ-infested object, such as a garbage can. Through therapy, the patient would learn to look at or handle the dirty object without being allowed to clean it. During this process, the patient would learn to confront his or her obsessions—the ulitmate goal being to enable the sufferer to gain the ability to deal with the anxiety associated with the objects that he or she is obsessing over.

Medications

Certain medications can also be helpful in treating OCD. As we mentioned, Prozac, which enhances the level of serotonin in the brain, is often prescribed for obsessive-compulsive disorder. Other useful medications include BuSpar, an antianxiety medication, and Clomipramine, an older antidepressant.

It can take up to three months for these medications to reach their full effectiveness. Medications and behavior therapy often complement each other. While medications alter the body's level of serotonin, behavior therapy helps the patient learn to resist compulsions and obsessive thoughts.

Coping with OCD

To the casual observer, an OCD sufferer might appear to be a highly efficient, fully functioning person. But to close observers, such as family members, the OCD sufferer looks more like someone mysteriously enslaved by forces beyond his or her control. If you suspect that your parent has OCD, you may have noticed some of the following behavioral patterns:

- Persistent lateness or absence from work and other appointments

- Constant questioning and need for reassurance
- Difficulty completing simple tasks in a reasonable amount of time
- Increased concern over details
- Extreme emotional reactions to insignificant events
- Inability to sleep properly
- Staying up late to get things done
- Change in eating habits
- Avoidance of certain things or situations
- Performance of usual routine becomes difficult

When "Helping" Your Parent Backfires

People with untreated OCD often find themselves increasingly isolated from others as a result of being preoccupied with their terrible thoughts and urges. Often, they choose to keep their illness a secret. This can be particularly difficult for families to deal with.

You might find yourself in the position of being the enabler for your OCD parent; in other words, you may actually find yourself doing the compulsive behavior for your parent just to keep the peace in your house or to keep your parent happy. Thus, it is important to remember that by trying to help your parent in the short-term, you may actually be hurting your parent (or even your whole family) in the long-term. What you think is "helping" your parent will only make your parent worse. Therefore, it is important that you don't try to "treat" your parent's OCD by yourself.

Don't Forget to Get Help for Yourself, Too

If you suspect that your parent has OCD, or if your parent has asked you to help with his/her compulsive behavior, talk to a trusted adult or medical professional who will be able to get your parent the help he or she needs. With treatment, most people experience a significant decrease in their symptoms of OCD. Your mental health professional may suggest that you attend a therapy session or a meeting with a therapist and your parent for support.

Always remember that as much as your parent needs support, you need support, too. If you think that you can benefit by talking with others who share this problem, there are support groups and other resources for family and friends available through county, state, and some private mental health associations (see the back of this book for more information).

Educate Yourself

Learning about OCD in general can help you and your family understand more about the disease. Ask your mental health professional if he or she can recommend any sources of information; your local library may have videos and audiotapes on the subject.

For many people, the thought of having an illness is far worse than the reality. Your parent—as well as yourself and the rest of your family—will be relieved to find that there is a name for the illness he or she suffers from, and that there are ways to treat it.

7 Substance Abuse

Many people who suffer from a mental illness frequently turn to alcohol and illegal substances to help them cope or to temporarily make themselves feel better. Substances like alcohol may seem to briefly alleviate a bad mood and other symptoms of depression—such as loss of energy, appetite, and sleep; however, often the substance abuse will mask the mental illness. As the child of a parent with mental illness, you may have noticed that your parent is abusing substances.

Using or Abusing

How can you tell if your parent is abusing substances and not just using them? Some families are uncomfortable with any use of alcohol, while others are used to having a glass of wine at dinner or a few beers at a party. Whatever the case, the person with a substance dependency disorder will show some or all of the following signs:

- Many failed attempts to cut down or stop using the substance

- ⇨ Taking the substance in larger amounts than originally intended
- ⇨ Using the substance over a longer period than intended
- ⇨ Continuing to use the substance despite voicing a persistent desire to stop
- ⇨ Not going to work, missing appointments, etc. because of being high or hung over
- ⇨ Foregoing activities and instead devoting time to the substance in question
- ⇨ Continuing to use the substance, despite significant negative consequences (such as driving while intoxicated)
- ⇨ Developing withdrawal symptoms when not using the substance
- ⇨ Developing a tolerance of the substance (using more and more of the substance to get the desired effect)

If some of these signs have lasted for at least a month or have occurred repeatedly over a longer period of time, there is cause for concern. If left untreated, your parent's substance abuse can lead to addiction. What can you do if you suspect that your parent is using substances to mask or deal with his/her mental illness? Ask another adult for help or speak with your family doctor. As with the signs and symptoms of mental illness, it will be helpful for you to educate yourself about substance abuse. Your school or local library should have numerous books on this subject.

Many people with substance abuse problems become defensive or angry when the subject is broached. Try not to worry if you confront your parent and he or she does not want to seek help right away. Your parent may be embarrassed about having a substance abuse problem he or she may be in denial about it.

Karen's Dad, Louis

Louis suffers from panic disorder. His attacks occur frequently and without warning, but they tend to happen when he is in crowded places, such as elevators. Louis found that by having a drink or two, he could lower his anxiety level, which seemed to decrease his fear of having panic attacks. But what started out as a drink or two after dinner turned into many drinks throughout the day. "Rationally, I knew it was wrong of me to cover up my feelings and fears with alcohol," says Louis. "But at the time, I wanted a 'quick fix'—something that would help ease my fears, something that I could do quickly and that wouldn't involve too much effort. But most of all, I wanted something that I could do on my own. I didn't have to go to a therapist and admit to my embarrassing problem. All I had to do was have a couple of drinks."

Louis's family was very concerned. "I suspected that my dad might have a drinking problem," admits Karen, Louis's daughter. "But I wasn't sure if it was a big problem, or if he just liked to have a drink or two. Also, I was embarrassed by the whole thing. I thought that it might just go away on its own. After a while, though, we realized that it was something we were going to have to deal with as a family."

Karen's family sat down with Louis and had a long conversation about the issue. "When I got in my car after having a number of drinks, it was then that I realized that I had a problem and could no longer deny it—I needed help. Drunk driving is an issue I have always felt passionate about, and here I was, about to drive under the influence." Louis's family did some research, and Louis found a therapist. They also decided that the entire family should begin attending group therapy sessions to help them get through this difficult time and to help deal with some of the issues associated with Louis's panic disorder and substance abuse.

8 Suicide

In the United States, suicide accounts for at least 25,000 deaths per year. Many people with mental illness are unable to cope with their feelings and with what they are going through. People often view suicide as a "way out"—they feel that they cannot cope with the reality of their situation anymore, and that suicide is the only option available to them.

Fortunately, there are often many warning signs to look out for. All threats or signs of suicide should be taken seriously. Some people think that when a person talks about attempting suicide, he or she is just doing so to get attention. If your parent, or anyone else you know, frequently talks about suicide or refers to it, do not assume that that person is just joking around. Listen to his or her concerns and recommend that he or she get professional help, or talk to an adult who will be able to help you with the situation.

Warning Signs

The following are some of the warning signs that a person may be considering suicide:

- Loses interest in activities and hobbies that were previously sources of pleasure.

- Gives away favorite possessions, such as stamp collections, jewelry, or money.

- Writes a will.

- Makes references to others who have died; although the death may have been tragic, there is a sense of identification or commiseration with the victim.

- Writes poetry and stories, or creates artwork that includes images of death and that indicates that he or she is suffering from profound loneliness.

- Continuously and persistently discounts the positive, choosing instead to focus on the negative.

- Increases alcohol or drug abuse.

- Makes preparations and/or talks about a suicide plan that is concrete, specific, within means, and lethal—and there are no deterrents to prevent carrying out the plan. This is a sign of great danger.

- Seems detached from emotions and withdraws from friends or family.

You should also know that asking questions about suicide does not put ideas into someone's head. In other words, bringing the subject up will not cause a person to commit suicide. And if you recognize any of the above warning signs in your parent, remember that mental illness is a medical illness, and that help is available. The most important thing that you can do for a loved one is to get professional help quickly so that he or she can begin his or her road to recovery.

When You Seek Help: What the Doctor Will Ask

If you suspect that your parent is contemplating suicide, speak with a mental health professional or another adult who will be able to help. A doctor will likely ask your parent some or all of the following questions:

- Have you been thinking a lot about death?
- Have you been wishing that you were dead or that you wouldn't wake up in the morning?
- Have you had thoughts about hurting yourself or killing someone?
- Have you made a plan to hurt yourself?

Find Out More About Suicide

You will find it helpful to educate yourself about suicide; begin by speaking with a doctor who can listen to and talk through your concerns. You should also consider taking out some books on the subject. These resources should help you answer your questions in detail and will help you realize that you are not alone. Your parent's doctor may offer some suggestions about how to deal with your situation—such as opening up the lines of communication in your family.

When Your Parent Is Not Cooperative

Keep in mind, though, that your parent may not be as receptive to communicating about his or her suicidal thoughts as you would like. Your parent might respond with anger or may be on the defensive—even if he or she does actually have suicidal thoughts, it can be a hard thing to admit. Your parent might feel ashamed or even guilty that these thoughts exist. A medical professional will be able to get your parent the help he or she needs.

Always Seek Help—It's There for You, Too

Perhaps you are not at the stage of identifying whether your parent might be suicidal. Perhaps your parent has already committed suicide or has a made a suicide attempt. In either of these cases, you should try your best to find ways to deal with all of the complicated feelings that this will stir up. Even if you would rather retreat and be on your own, you may find it to be more helpful in the long run if you talk about your issues with a counselor or medical professional.

There are many support groups available that can help you realize that you are not alone, and that many people are experiencing similar feelings. You need the support and comfort of others—both family and friends—as well as professional guidance. Be sure to reach out to others if you need help

As the offspring of a suicidal parent, you are probably feeling a wide range of emotions, including blaming yourself, thinking that you could have prevented it, or wondering what you did wrong. Individual and family psychotherapy can help you realize that none of these things are true. Through therapy, you can also learn effective coping techniques that will help you come to terms with a loved one's suicide attempt. Be sure to get help for yourself during this difficult time; you should not try to go through this alone.

Finding the Right Help

Finding the right help for your parent can be a hard thing to do. As has been mentioned throughout this book, the best thing for you to do is to speak with a trusted adult or medical professional who will be able to help you with the situation. However, whenever possible, choosing the right mental health professional should be handled by another adult who can take control of the situation.

Regardless of the particular mental illness your parent has, it will be helpful for you to find out more about the disease. Go to the library and contact the relevant organizations in your area (some of these are listed at the end of this book). Read everything you can: pamphlets, books, magazines, and newsletters. This will give you a solid foundation on which to build your knowledge as you go forward.

You can also contact the organizations listed at the back of this book for more information and advice. You may find that you are feeling overwhelmed and are having a hard time dealing with everything involved with having a mentally ill parent. If you are feeling this way, pay special attention to this chapter.

Although you should not be responsible for choosing a mental health professional for your parent, the following are some of the options your parent has. As you will see, there are numerous resources for getting further information and recommendations. The list below can also be of some help to you if you and other family members choose to talk to someone.

- Your family doctor or a religious or spiritual advisor
- Friends and other family members
- Local psychiatric and psychological societies
- Local or state affiliates of national organizations
- Senior citizen centers or family service/social service agencies
- Your insurance company or HMO, which may have a list of participating therapists that you can choose from
- Private or state hospitals with outpatient clinics
- A nearby university or teaching hospital that has a counseling center or a psychiatry/psychology professor specializing in your parent's illness (if you already have a diagnosis)
- Community mental health centers, where services are often available at low cost or on a sliding fee scale for people who are unable to pay high fees

Your Family Doctor and Other Professionals

Many people first consult their family doctor, as it is important to rule out any physical illness that could be causing your parent's symptoms. But family doctors are often not trained to recognize or deal with mental problems. Below is a list of professionals who are trained in dealing with mental illness.

Psychiatrists

Psychiatrists are physicians (M.D.s) who have graduated from medical school and have completed four additional years of training in psychiatry. In general, they are the only mental health professionals permitted to prescribe medication. Some psychiatrists focus on medications and deal exclusively with individuals that have severe and persistent mental illnesses, while others conduct psychotherapy and prescribe medication.

Psychologists

Psychologists have completed master's degrees and doctorates in psychology or counseling. Their degrees may read Ph.D., Psy.D., or Ed.D. Working with individuals, families, and children, they may be trained in many forms of therapy and must undergo two years of supervised internship after the completion of their doctorate.

Clinical Social Workers

Social workers hold master's degrees (and sometimes Ph.D.s). Their training includes fieldwork in a wide range of human services, including mental health settings. They often focus on the social context of their patients' lives. In most states, licensed clinical social workers (L.C.S.W. or C.S.W.) are required to undergo supervised training before they can conduct therapy with individuals and families.

Psychiatric Nurses

Psychiatric nurses are registered nurses with additional training in psychiatry. They often work in mental health settings as part of a therapeutic team. Advanced practice nurses hold master's degrees and can provide psychotherapy, and in some states they may be allowed to prescribe medication.

Marriage and Family Therapists

These professionals usually hold master's degrees and have undergone supervised training. If you are considering seeing a marriage or family therapist, be sure that he or she is licensed. In many states, anyone can offer marriage therapy or marriage counseling, even if he or she has not had the appropriate training.

Clergy

Pastoral counselors can offer psychological counseling within a religious context. They are not required to be licensed, but they may have received additional psychological training and may be certified by the American Association of Pastoral Counselors.

Check the Qualifications of Your Mental Health Practitioner

It is important to keep in mind that anyone can be called a psychotherapist; it is not a legal term. Whether you are seeking the help for yourself or for your parent, the mental health professional you choose should be licensed by your state. This assures you that the individual has had extensive training and supervised practice, that he or she has passed a state or national qualifying exam, and has pursued continuing education to help keep up to date with changes in the field. You should also ask if the individual is a member of the American Psychiatric Association, the American Psychological Association, or another nationally recognized group.

Finding the Right Therapist

There are many factors to consider when helping to choose a mental health professional for your parent. These include the severity of the illness, your parent's preference for medication or psychotherapy (or both), and your family's financal situation.

If it has been decided that your parent needs therapy, the search may take some time. Some people "shop" for a therapist, interviewing several before choosing one. Keep in mind that if a therapist isn't working out for your parent and/or family, you can always choose a new one. The process of getting well involves many adjustments in treatment, including finding new doctors and other people who can help.

When to Get Help for Yourself

Perhaps your parent has been suffering from a mental illness that was diagnosed by a professional some time ago, and he or she is being treated with therapy and/or medication. Or perhaps you suspect that your parent is mentally ill, but as of yet, you have not sought help, and your parent has not been officially diagnosed. Regardless of where your parent is in the treatment process, you may decide that you need to find a support group for yourself.

Knowing the details of the illness—why your parent refuses treatment or why a certain treatment does not seem to be working very well—can help you cope with the day-to-day results of the disease. A mental health professional, or other people in a support group who are going through the same things you are going through, can help give you the specific advice that you need.

Remember Your Needs

It is important for you to remember that you have needs as well. You may be spending your entire day completely focused on your parent's illness, making sure that he or she feels better. This can be exhausting. Consider getting help for yourself during this difficult period in your life, regardless of whether or not your parent is in treatment.

Your Options

There are many options available to you if you decide to seek help for yourself. If your parent is already in therapy, you might want to consider attending a session or two with him or her. However, some people are not open to this possibility because of the sensitive nature of the topics being discussed. There are many other possibilities. You might choose individual psychotherapy, family therapy, group therapy, or a support group.

Individual psychotherapy can help you deal with the strong feelings that you might have about your parent's illness. It can also help you learn how to deal and communicate more effectively with your parent. Family therapy can help you and your parent or family communicate more constructively and learn how to problem-solve as a team. Group therapy or a support group can help you realize that you are not alone in the struggle to deal with your parent's illness. You can learn many things from other people who have been in similar situations.

Coming to Terms with Your Emotions

The children of mentally ill parents often experience a confusingly wide range of emotions. You will likely feel worry and concern for your parent, but you may also experience anger, embarrassment, guilt, and disgust. Some children of parents with mental illness spend time wishing the whole thing—even the parent—would just go away. After all, being young is hard enough without having to deal with a difficult family situation.

Try to remember that these feelings are all normal. It is natural for you to be embarrassed if your friends ask you what is wrong with your parent, just as it is normal to feel guilty if you wish that your parent would disappear. Many children of mentally ill parents find it helpful to speak with a therapist about their feelings and concerns; doing so can help you further realize that you are not alone.

In addition to professional help, it is important to let others know how you are doing. Talk to a teacher, a relative, your guidance counselor, or a friend. You will find it very helpful to have social support as you go through this difficult time with your parent and family.

Helpful Coping Strategies

As you go through this tough and trying time, you may find it extremely useful to keep various coping strategies in mind. You may be in the stage of suspecting that your parent has a mental illness, or in the stage of helping your parent with his or her treatment, or in the stage of adapting to new routines. No matter what the particulars of your situation are, you may find that the suggestions below are helpful to you.

Be Realistic

At the very start, you may feel as though you will be able to handle your parent's illness by yourself. However, you will need to be realistic about this. For example, you may know of a few ways that you can lift your parent's spirits or a few techniques for making everything seem a little bit better. But no matter how skilled you are, you will not be able to cope on your own: Your parent needs you, but your parent also needs professional help. Be realistic in your expectations of yourself and about the help you can provide, but also be realistic about the help provided by a professional. Treatment will take time—and it won't be easy.

Keep Your Routine

As you, your parent, and your family try to cope, your normal family routine may be disrupted. You might find yourself going to school late, or cutting short your activities outside of the home so that you can be around your parent more often. While it would be impossible to try to keep the exact same routine that you had before your parent became ill, try to stick with your routine as much as possible. This will help provide structure during an unstructured, and often hectic, time.

Don't Take It Personally

It is difficult for all of us to watch a parent in pain. As our parent's children, we often think that we are responsible for our parent's moods, or that we are to blame when something goes wrong. While this type of thinking is normal, it is important to remember that you are not responsible for your parent's illness—much in the same way that you would not be responsible if your parent had a cavity or a sprained ankle.

There are certain things that are outside of our control; while you can help your parent, you can't fix his or her illness, and you are not responsible for it. As previously mentioned, you will likely feel a wide variety of emotions as you go through this difficult time; these feelings are normal.

Share Your Feelings

It can be very valuable to share your feelings and experiences with your parent, a friend, an adult, and/or a therapist. Try to remember that others care about you and would like to listen to what you are going through. Many people are surprised to find out that the people around them are supportive and can offer good advice.

Ask for Help

It is important to remember that mental illnesses do not have simple cures. While you can help your parent with what he or she is going through and provide necessary support, you will not be able to cure the disease. Remember that your parent needs help, but so do you. Speak with a therapist, family member, or friend about anything that you need help with.

Coping with a parent who is mentally ill will likely be one of the most difficult experiences you ever have. Every stage of the illness—be it pre-diagnosis, during treatment, or after treatment—will be difficult, and will present its own set of challenges. While you are in a unique position to help, support, and encourage your parent, you must also remember that you have feelings and emotions of your own to deal with.

Try your best to continue doing the activities you enjoy; continue spending time with your friends. Many people find it helpful to take up a hobby or an activity that they did not previously engage in; this can help take your mind off the weightier issues that you are dealing with.

Just remember that no one expects you to go through this alone—and you shouldn't, either.

The following pages list some helpful resources for you: organizations, Web sites, and books. All contain important information and advice that can help you, your family, and your parent get educated and stay informed.

Glossary

agoraphobia Condition in which the afflicted person is afraid of open or public spaces.

amygdala Almond-shaped region in the brain that is involved in deciding whether or not a noise or sight we experience is worthy of a fearful reaction.

antidepressant Medicine that is used to fix chemical imbalances in the brain.

anxiety disorder The most common class of mental illnesses—includes panic disorder, phobias, and obsessive-compulsive disorder.

asylum Institution for the care of the mentally ill or the aged.

bipolar disorder Mental illness in which people have extreme mood swings that alternate from depression to mania.

catatonia Symptom of schizophrenia in which the patient may grimace or adopt strange facial expressions.

catatonic immobility Symptom of schizophrenia in which the patient adopts unusual postures and maintains them for long periods of time.

cortex Major part of the brain's gray matter that is involved in sensing, moving, and thinking.

delusion False belief, in spite of invalidating evidence.

depression Condition marked by an inability to concentrate, insomnia, and feelings of dejection and guilt.

dopamine Neurotransmitter in the brain that regulates movement and influences mood and motivation.

electroconvulsive therapy (ECT) Procedure in which the patient receives mild electrical stimulation of the brain.

endocrine system Controls the production and functioning of the body's hormones.

epilepsy Disorder marked by recurring motor, sensory, or psychic malfunctions with or without consciousness or convulsive movements.

exposure therapy Technique used in cognitive behavioral therapy in which a patient is slowly exposed to a fearful situation until he or she becomes desensitized to it.

genetic predisposition When a person is more likely to have a disease because of a genetic link.

hallucination False or distorted perception of objects or events that the patient mistakes for reality.

hemorrhage Excessive bleeding from the blood vessels.

hypomania Condition experienced by people with bipolar disorder in which the mania experienced is less pronounced and symptoms are not as exaggerated.

irritable bowel syndrome Condition characterized by intermittent bouts of gastrointestinal cramps and diarrhea or constipation.

mania Condition experienced by people with bipolar disorder, in which the individual goes through an emotional state of intense elation.

manic depression Another term for bipolar disorder; see definition of bipolar disorder.

neurotransmitters Chemical messengers that transmit electrical signals from one nerve cell to another.

norepinephrine Neurotransmitter, that is, a vasoconstrictor found naturally in the body's sympathetic nerve endings, the deficit of which is often linked to mental illness.

obsessive-compulsive disorder (OCD) Illness characterized by a tendency to dwell on unwanted thoughts or ideas, or by the tendency perform repetitive rituals.

prefrontal cortex Part of the brain located in the frontal lobe. This part of our brain is called the "working memory."

psychosis Severe mental disorder characterized by the degeneration of normal intellectual and social functioning and by complete or partial withdrawal from society.

psychotherapy Treatment of mental illness that involves interaction between a patient and a therapist. The most common type of psychotherapy involves speaking with a health-care professional about past experiences, relationships, thoughts, and feelings.

rapid cycling Condition experienced by people with bipolar disorder in which mood swings occur almost continuously.

schizophrenia Condition marked by withdrawal from reality with accompanying affective, behavioral, and intellectual disturbances.

serotonin Neurotransmitter—the deficit of which is often linked to mental illness—that is active in vasoconstriction and the transmission of nerve impulses.

stress Mental, emotional, or physical tension, strain, or distress.

substance abuse Excessive use of addictive substances, such as alcohol and narcotic drugs.

suicide Act of intentionally killing oneself.

support group Group of people, sometimes led by a therapist, who provide each other with moral support, information, and advice on problems relating to a shared characteristic or experience.

tardive dyskinesia Condition experienced by some schizophrenic patients who are using neuroleptics, in which a person experiences involuntary movements, such as lip smacking and facial grimacing.

thalamus Part of the brain that helps filter, process, and relay input from the senses, emotions, and memory.

therapist Specialist in the treatment of illness or disability.
ventricles Fluid-filled spaces in the brain.
waxy flexibility Symptom of schizophrenia in which another person can move a patient's limbs into strange positions that will be maintained for long periods of time.

Where to Go for Help

In the United States

American Association for Marriage and Family Therapy
1133 15th Street NW, Suite 300
Washington, DC 20005-2710
(202) 452-0109
Web site: http://www.aamft.org

American Foundation for Suicide Prevention
120 Wall Street, 22nd floor
New York, NY 10005
(212) 363-3500
(888) 333-2377
Web site: http://www.afsp.org

American Medical Association (AMA)
515 North State Street
Chicago, IL 60610
(312) 464-5000
Web site: http://www.ama-assn.org

American Psychiatric Association
1400 K Street NW
Washington, DC 20005

(202) 682-6066
(800) 368-5777
Web site: http://www.psych.org

American Psychological Association (APA)
750 First Street NE
Washington, DC 20002-4242
(800) 374-2721
(202) 336-5500
Web site: http://www.apa.org

Anxiety Disorders Association of America
11900 Parklawn Drive, Suite 100
Rockville, MD 20852
(301) 231-9350
Web site: http://www.adaa.org

Freedom from Fear
308 Seaview Avenue
Staten Island, NY 10305
(718) 351-1717
Web site: http://www.freedomfromfear.org

Lithium Information Center
Madison Institute of Medicine
7617 Mineral Point Road, Suite 300
Madison, WI 53717
(608) 827-2470
Web site: http://www.healthtechsys.com/mimlithium.html

National Alliance for the Mentally Ill (NAMI)
Colonial Place Three
2107 Wilson Boulevard, Suite 300
Arlington, VA 22203

(703) 524-7600
(800) 829-8289
Web site: http://www.nami.org/narsad

National Alliance for Research on Schizophrenia and Depression (NARSAD)
60 Cutter Mill Road, Suite 404
Great Neck, NY 11021
(516) 829-0091
Web site: http://www.mhsource.com

National Depressive and Manic-Depressive Association (NDMDA)
730 North Franklin Street, Suite 501
Chicago, IL 60610-3632
(312) 642-0049
(800) 826-3632
Web site: http://www.ndmda.org

National Foundation for Depressive Illness (NAFDI)
P.O. Box 2257
New York, NY 10116
(800) 239-1265
Web site: http://www.depression.org

National Institute of Mental Health (NIMH)
6001 Executive Boulevard, Room 8184, MSC 9663
Bethesda, MD 20892-9663
(301) 443-4513
(800) 421-4211
Web site: http://www.nimh.nih.gov

National Mental Health Association
1021 Prince Street

Alexandria, VA 22314-2971
(800) 969-NMHA (6642)
Web site: http://www.nmha.org

Obsessive-Compulsive Foundation (OCF)
337 Notch Hill Road
North Branford, CT 06471
(203) 315-2190
Web site: http://www.ocfoundation.org

Obsessive Compulsive Information Center
Madison Institute of Medicine
7617 Mineral Point Road, Suite 300
Madison, WI 53717
(608) 827-2470
Web site: http://www.healthtechsys.com/mimocic.html

In Canada

Canadian Mental Health Association
2160 Yonge Street, 3rd floor
Toronto, ON M4S 2Z3
(416) 484-7750
E-mail: cmhanat@interlog.com
Web site: http://www.cmha.ca

Canadian Public Health Association
1565 Carling Avenue, Suite 400
Ottawa, ON K1Z 8R1
(613) 725-3769
Web site: http://www.cpha.ca

Canadian Red Cross Society
170 Metcalfe Street
Ottawa, ON K2P 2P2

(613) 740-1900
Web site: http://www.redcross.ca

Canadian Traumatic Stress Network
1018 3rd Street East
Saskatoon, SK S7H 1M9
(866) 288-CTSN (2876)
Web site: http://www.ctsn-rcst.ca

Centre Pyscho-Social Pour Enfants et Familles
500 rue Old St. Patrick
Ottawa, ON K1N 9G4
(613) 789-2240
Web site: http://www.synapse.net

Family Service Canada
Services á la Famille
383 Parkdale
Ottawa, ON K1Y 4R4
(613) 722-9006
Web site: http://www.familyservicecanada.org

Madness and Arts World Festival
Workman Theatre Project
1001 Queen Street West
Toronto, ON MJ6 1HY
(416) 583-4339

Web Sites

British Columbia Schizophrenia Society
http://www.bcssvictoria.gq.nu

Centre for Addiction and Mental Health
http://www.camh.net

Depression.com
http://www.depression.com

Internet Mental Health
http://www.mentalhealth.com

Pendulum Resources—Bipolar Disorders Portal
http://www.pendulum.org

The Society for Manic Depression
http://www.societymd.org

Wing of Madness Depression Community
http://www.wingofmadness.com

For Further Reading

Amador, Xavier. *I Am Not Sick! I Don't Need Help.* Peconic, NY: 2000.

Babior, Shirley, and Carol Goldman. *Overcoming Panic, Anxiety, and Phobias: New Strategies to Free Yourself from Worry and Fear.* Duluth, MN: Pfeifer-Hamilton, 1996.

Dumont, Raeann. *The Sky is Falling: Understanding and Coping with Phobias, Panic, and Obsessive-Compulsive Disorders.* New York: W.W. Norton and Co., 1996.

Feniger, Mani. *Journey from Anxiety to Freedom: Moving Beyond Panic and Phobias and Learning to Trust Yourself.* Rocklin, CA: Prima Publishing, 1997.

Friedman, Michele S. *Everything You Need to Know About Schizophrenia.* New York: The Rosen Publishing Group, Inc., 2000

Fran, Renee. *What Happened to Mommy?* New York: R.D. Eastman Publishing, 1994.

Gorman, Jack M. *The Essential Guide to Psychiatric Drugs, 3rd ed.* New York: St. Martin's Press, 1997.

Karp, David Allen. *The Burden of Sympathy: How Families Cope with Mental Illness.* New York: Oxford University Press, 2001.

Marsh, Diane T. *How to Cope with Mental Illness in Your Family: A Self-Care Guide for Siblings, Offspring, and Parents.* New York: J.P. Tarcher, 1998.

Lark, Susan. *Dr. Susan Lark's Anxiety and Stress Self Help Book.* Berkeley, CA: Celestial Arts, 1996.

Peurifoy, Reneau Z. *Overcoming Anxiety: From Short-Term Fixes to Long-Term Recovery.* New York: Henry Holt and Co., 1997.

Potter, Beverly. *The Worrywart's Companion: Twenty-One Ways to Soothe Yourself and Worry Smart.* Berkeley, CA: Wildcat Canyon Press, 1997.

Sapolsky, Robert M. *Why Zebras Don't Get Ulcers: An Updated Guide to Stress, Stress-Related Diseases, and Coping.* New York: W.H. Freeman and Co., 1998.

Sommers, Michael A. *Everything You Need to Know About Bipolar Disorder and Manic Depressive Illness.* New York: The Rosen Publishing Group, Inc., 2000.

Wainwright, Tabitha. *You and An Illness in Your Family.* New York: The Rosen Publishing Group, Inc., 2001.

Weiden, Peter J. *Breakthroughs in Antipsychotic Medications: A Guide for Consumers, Families, and Clinitions.* New York: W.W. Norton & Company, 2000.

Index

C

D

E

F

G

H

I

About the Author

Allison J. Ross graduated with degrees in English and psychology. She currently lives in Manhattan, where she works in public relations. This is her seventh book for young adults.